FAITHFUL
& TRUE

KRISTI MENASHE

He is always faithful!

Lam. 3:22-23

♡ *Kristi Menashe*

Faithful & True:
Devotions and Prayers on the Attributes of God

Copyright © 2023 by Kristi Menashe

ISBN: 9798856315775

Cover design and internal formatting: Brittany Castellano

Unless otherwise indicated, all Scripture quotations are taken from the Holy Bible, New King James Version. Copyright © 1982 by Thomas Nelson, Inc.. Used by permission. All rights reserved.

Any emphases in Scripture quotations have been added by the author.

All formal definitions are taken from the American Dictionary of the English Language (Noah Webster, 1828).

My Heart, Christ's Home (Robert Boyd Munger, 1986) (Jealous)

Instruments In The Redeemer's Hands (Paul David Tripp, 2002) (Jealous)

Come & Adore (Kristi Menashe, 2020) (Active)

Instruments In The Redeemer's Hands (Paul David Tripp, 2002) (Loving)

TO MY LORD AND SAVIOR, JESUS CHRIST-

Thank You for saving a wretch like me. Thank You for using a wretch like me. Thank You for giving me this beautiful life, that I am so unworthy of. Most of all, thank You for being a: faithful, sovereign, personal, good, sufficient, able, available, patient, wonderful, omnipresent, gracious, merciful, majestic, generous, omnipotent, trustworthy, jealous, great, active, wise, holy, righteous, strong, loving, praiseworthy, unchanging, marvelous, just, omniscient, eternal, and true God. I am in awe of You and I will never stop sharing. To know You and to make You known are the desires of my heart...

TO MY HUSBAND AND HERO, JOSH-

Thank you for being my tangible representation of Christ. Thank you for loving me like Jesus loves me. Thank you for always encouraging me, for protecting me, and for always helping me fulfill the callings the Lord has put upon my life. Thank you for investing in me and in our children. Thank you for adventuring with us. Thank you for daily laying down your life: for me, for the kids, and for others. My friends ask where you keep your cape...and they're right in seeing you as a superhero. How does God love me so much that He chose to give you to me?! I am forever grateful He did. You are my greatest gift, and you have my heart for all of my days...

TO MY FOUR PRECIOUS ARROWS-

Thank you for teaching me...always. Thank you for forgiving me when I mess up, and for loving me despite my failures and shortcomings as a mom. My utmost desire is to point you four to Jesus, and to spend eternity with you. I am so very proud of each of you. The Lord shows me so much about His own (perfect) character as I parent you. He gently reveals where I need reproof, correction, and instruction in righteousness. (2 Timothy 3:16-17) He has given me the privilege and responsibility of training you, and I don't take my job lightly. You are my God-given gifts and rewards. (Psalm 127:3) I hope and pray that you'll choose

Him— always and forever. Even when you see my sin. Even as you live with my flaws. His love covers, and I am so thankful that, though I'll never be the perfect parent, our God always is! He loves you even more than I do. I pray you'll continue to follow Him, delight in Him, and enjoy His rich blessings— as long as He ordains.

TO BRAVE AND BEAUTIFUL TAYLOR-

You are a true beauty, inside and out. I see a quiet faith, strength, gentleness, and dignity in you that is a rarity. You're a blessing to our family, and you've become like a daughter to us. In our wildest dreams, we could never have imagined what the Lord had planned and how He would forever connect our families. We feel privileged to be part of your life and your story. We love every moment spent with you. We pray for you always and we look forward to what the Lord has in store for you. He has used you in mighty ways for His kingdom purposes (and I have a feeling He is just getting started). Keep shining for Him. Keep pointing others to Him. Keep trusting Him. "I liver you!"

TO MIGHTY AND DETERMINED MIKAH-

You are such a brave boy! We have loved you all of your life, and it has been a joy to watch you grow! We have rejoiced with you and your family in your healing and we have pleaded with the Lord to "do it again." We hate watching you battle cancer. You truly amaze and astound everyone around you! God has gifted you in many ways, and your athletic ability (even while undergoing treatment) is incredible. We have made so many fun memories with you and your family and we can't wait to make more. The Lord is going to use you and your story for His glory and purposes! God is alive and active in your life and I look forward to what He has yet to do...

INTRODUCTION

In the summer of 2020, my husband, Josh, and I were made aware of a dire situation. A friend ("D") from church needed a kidney transplant. The two of us began to go through the testing process, to see if either of us would be a suitable match for her. After filling out online forms and then going to Loma Linda for bloodwork, we waited. After a few days had passed, we each received calls from the hospital. I will never forget that day. "You're a match!" said the woman on the other end. I began to cry as a tidal wave of emotions hit. Her voice was compassionate. "It's a big decision. Talk to your husband. Think about it." I then asked about Josh… "Is my husband a match too?" She told me she wasn't allowed to give me that answer, but that she had spoken with him already and that I should call him right away. I knew right then that he was also a match. I called Josh as soon as I hung up the phone and we both just started crying. He insisted that he would be the donor. Josh felt strongly that he was to be the one to move forward in the process. Within a few days, he called Loma Linda and he also called D's husband…to share the good news. I think they were in shock, and I know they were extremely grateful. The hospital quickly sent Josh the supplies for the next tests in the process but then he spoke with D's husband again. Josh was told he should wait before moving forward. Long story short— D's sister was a match as well, and in January of 2021, they both underwent surgery. Praise God…it was successful and they're both healthy and doing well today!

We had no idea at that time that the Lord was just preparing our hearts for something big to come! He used that "Abraham" situation (where He wanted to see if we would obey, but didn't require the sacrifice) to do a work in Josh and in me…

My best friend, Leah, had introduced us to a sweet and beautiful young woman named Taylor. Taylor had been battling fibrolamellar carcinoma, a rare cancer of the liver, for over four years. By the time we met her in person, our family had already been praying for her that entire time. During that summer of 2020, when she was feeling up for it— Taylor, Debi (Taylor's mom), Leah, and I would hike a local trail. It was then that I got to know Taylor a little better...and was able to gain more insight into her ongoing fight against cancer.

In the summer of 2021, Taylor and I were chatting via Instagram when she told me she would (possibly) be needing a live liver donor. Because my husband is a universal blood donor and the most brave man I know, I wrote Taylor and told her that Josh would be willing to see if he would be a match for her. (Later that day, I told Josh I had "offered" him and, of course, he was totally good with it!) Taylor and I chatted a few more times and then came a day when she asked if she and her parents could come over and talk to us about what being a donor would entail.

Taylor, Rick, and Debi came over on a hot summer night in August of 2021. Taylor's perfectly polished nails, tiny frame, and big smile didn't give away the fact that she was very sick... but her jaundiced skin did. As the three of them sat on our couch and shared about the transplant Taylor needed, Josh's heart was touched in a big way. We fought tears, and as they left that night— he was already prepared to fill out the necessary online forms. Josh says that seeing Tay's dad hurting for his girl is what really struck him. He couldn't imagine being in that position— as a father...feeling helpless but not hopeless.

From that point on, it was a bit of a whirlwind. One day, maybe the Lord will call me to write a book about all of the intricate and intimate details. On October 1, 2021, Josh and Taylor underwent liver transplant surgery. Taylor was given 65% of Josh's liver and a great big piece of his heart and mine. We can both say our lives will never be the same, after such a life-changing experience. I didn't get cut open that day…but in the days leading up to surgery, and in the days that followed, I got a front row seat— as I got to watch God's goodness, grace, and mercy in Taylor's life unfold.

At this point, you might be wondering why I am sharing all of this in the introduction of a book about God and His attributes…

As Josh and I arrived back home after two weeks of being in Pittsburgh, Pennsylvania for the surgery and initial recovery, I was truly in awe of God— in a brand new way. As I watched my husband heal and assimilate back to "normal" life, we continued to pray for Taylor and get daily updates. That first month after surgery was very difficult for Taylor…and her body fought hard! Yet, through her struggles and physical pain, Taylor continued to have a deep faith.

My faith grew exponentially during this time. It didn't matter what happened to us or around us— I just knew God would provide what was needed. I knew He would reveal Himself. I knew He would answer. I knew He would remain faithful…and true to His Word.

Taylor's name is mentioned throughout this devotional, along with references to Josh and to the surgery. I felt it necessary (and crucial) for you to know and understand how this book came to be.

As November of 2021 began (exactly one month after the surgery), God stirred my heart to thank Him for an attribute of His each day. As I had done in the past (with Come & Adore: An Advent Devotional), I posted on Instagram. The Lord led and guided me to focus on one attribute each day. As you read, you will see that I have barely scratched the surface! What I have done is this: I've shared some personal examples of how the Lord worked in my life. I have shared verses and passages that tell of God's incredible character! I have attempted to lead you in prayer and in journaling— as you see God's attributes come to life in a real and deeply personal way.

Our God is infinite. We could search His Word every moment of every day for an entire lifetime…and still not have complete knowledge or understanding! There will never be a day where we will be able to say that we know all there is to know about Him. That might intimidate some, but I actually love that my relationship with the Lord will never be boring. There will always be new things I can learn about Him— even though He is the same yesterday, today, and forever.

If you don't know Jesus Christ as your Lord and Savior, I implore you to call out to Him. Ask Him to come and dwell in your heart. You will never regret giving your life to Christ. In love, I declare to you today that you are missing out on a full, exciting, abundant life…if Jesus isn't part of it. It's not easy to be a follower of Christ, but there is nothing more worthwhile.

Christ is all to me. My only Hope. The only Way, Truth, and Life. The One I will spend eternity with. If you'd like to invite Jesus into your heart and life today, go to Him in prayer.

Dear God…I recognize that I am a sinner in need of a Savior. I turn from my sin, and I need Your forgiveness. I believe that Your Son, Jesus, came to earth, lived a sinless life, and then died for me. He did what I couldn't do for myself. I ask You to come into my heart and life, and to take control. Thank You for Your mercy and grace. Thank You for Your great love for me. I want to live for You, in a way that is pleasing to You. I want to spend eternity with You! Come into my heart and life and have Your way in me. In Jesus' name, Amen.

(Eph. 2:8-9, Titus 3:5, Romans 10:9, Acts 4:12, John 14:6, Acts 16:30-33)

Christ went to the cross for you. He carried the weight of your sin. He died a brutal death for you. Jesus didn't stay dead, though. He rose to life and forever defeated the grave!

Maybe you do belong to Christ, but you are not feeling His goodness. I urge you to continue trusting. He never leaves nor forsakes us. We may distance ourselves from Him, but He never walks away from us! The Lord continues to remind me that He is always at work in the unseen. Don't lose heart. Don't give up hope.

There is coming a day…

Now I saw heaven opened, and behold, a white horse. And He who sat on him was called Faithful and True, and in righteousness He judges and wages war. His eyes were like a flame of fire, and on His head were many crowns. He had a name written that no one knew except Himself. He was clothed with a robe dipped in blood, and His name is called The Word of God. And the armies in heaven, clothed in fine linen, white and clean, followed Him on white horses. Now out of His mouth goes a sharp sword, that with it He should strike the nations. And He Himself will rule them with a rod of iron. He Himself treads the wine press of the fierceness and wrath of Almighty God. And He has on His robe and on His thigh a name written: KING OF KINGS AND LORD OF LORDS. (Revelation 19:11-16)

He knows and loves you.
He wants you to know Him, and to see His hand in everything.
He is faithful and He is true.

Until we see Him face to face, press on. Draw near(er) to the lover of your soul...

Looking forward to His glorious appearing and spending eternity with you, friends,

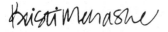

FAITHFUL

Thank You, God, that You are…faithful.

FAITHFUL

"Firmly adhering to duty; of true fidelity; loyal; constant in the performance of duties or services; observant of...contracts... vows; true to the marriage covenant; constant; not fickle; worthy of belief..."

Above is a short description from my favorite guy, Webster, of what it means to be faithful.

One of my most favorite passages in the Bible is from Lamentations...

Through the Lord's mercies we are not consumed, Because His compassions fail not. They are new every morning; Great is Your faithfulness. (Lam. 3:22-23)

If I had written that little portion of Scripture, I would have made those exclamatory sentences, ending them in exclamation marks!

How could we ever get over God's faithfulness?

He is loyal— even when we are disloyal, unfaithful, and wavering.

He is constant— even when we are inconsistent, fickle, wishy-washy, or vacillating.

He is true— even when we are incorrect, unauthentic, and hesitant.

1

He keeps His covenants— even when we break our promises.

As I was thinking upon God's faithfulness, a verse kept coming to mind: ... *"for He makes His sun rise on the evil and on the good, and sends rain on the just and on the unjust."* (Matthew 5:45b)

I guess what hits me is this: our God is faithful to His Word and to His promises, whether we keep our end of the bargain or not. He does what He says He will do. There is so much evil, wickedness, and perversion...yet God continues to allow the rain to fall, the sun to rise, the breath in our lungs.

Though we are often faithless, we get to enjoy His consistency. This is incredibly humbling for me.

The song Promises is often on repeat around here:

♪ God of Abraham...You're the God of covenant and faithful promises...Time and time again...You have proven You'll do just what You said...Great is Your faithfulness to me...From the rising sun to the setting same...I will praise Your name... Great is Your faithfulness to me! ♪

"All my life You have been faithful"...and all my life— You always will be.

Let us hold fast the confession of our hope without wavering, for He who promised is faithful. (Heb. 10:23)

PRAISE YOU, MY FAITHFUL GOD

You keep Your promises and You are faithful in everything. You promise that You will never leave me or forsake me. Even when I doubt, worry, or am afraid…You are constantly faithful to me. You hold me in the palm of Your hand and I need not fear. Because of Your faithfulness, I have every reason to trust You and surrender all to You. I lay everything at Your feet…and I put all of my hope in You and in Your unfailing word. Thank You for loving me. Thank You for being my Promise Keeper. I want to be more like You, Lord— one that keeps promises and stands by [her] word. Make me more like You, Jesus…

In Your Precious Name, Amen

HOW HAS GOD SHOWN HIS FAITHFULNESS IN YOUR LIFE?

_____

_____

_____

_____

_____

SOVEREIGN

Thank You, God, that You are...sovereign.

SOVEREIGN

My overwhelming need and desire to express my gratitude to God feels stronger during this month of thanks-giving...

For a long while now, the Lord will randomly remind me of His attributes and characteristics. I am overcome as He works in and through me. I am humbled as I realize that the One who possesses the highest power, and ALL authority and control (the ruler of all) wants to have a relationship with me!

When I am going to study something (in regards to the Bible/God/etc.), I get out my little library of commentaries, word studies, and dictionaries...and I dig in. It's always amazing to see which "nuggets" await.

In reading one of my Bible dictionaries this morning, I came to:

"God rules and works according to His eternal purpose, even through events that seem to contradict or oppose His rule."

Lately, more than any other attribute, it's His sovereignty that God reminds me of. I can't wrap my puny brain around it, because His sovereignty is far beyond human understanding. The crazy thing is that, as soon as I am astounded by God's sovereignty, I am undone by the fact that He's a God of infinite detail. A God who works in the biggest of ways and in the smallest of capacities. It's in the most minute intricacies that I am the most dumbfounded and awestruck. If you have a personal relationship with the Creator of the universe, you know exactly what I am referring to.

For I know that the Lord is great, And our Lord is above all gods. Whatever the Lord pleases He does, In heaven and in earth, In the seas and in the deep places. (Psalm 135:5-6)

I don't always like the way the Lord does (or doesn't do) things. I often pout, complain, cry, and whine…before submitting to His perfect will and plan, but:

There's a holy surrender that has to take place, as we lay all of our expectations at the feet of Jesus. There is a shift that must happen— in our hearts and minds, as we yield to His plans. There is a transfer of authority, as we humbly bow to His will. There is a childlike wonder, as our eyes are opened to His eternal purposes.

He is God. I am not. Sovereign over all. Praise You, Lord.

PRAISE YOU, MY SOVEREIGN GOD

Thank You that You are in complete control. Nothing surprises You! You hold the world and everything in it in the palm of Your righteous right hand. I praise You— for You are never caught off guard. You are provident and You know everything in advance. You allow and ordain every single thing that happens and because of that, I can rest in You. I can hope in You. I can trust in You. You are good and I will praise You all of my days. Lord, when fears arise or when I try to take matters into my own hands, please work in my heart and life. I give You the reins and I ask that You move mightily. I love You and praise Your sovereign name.

In Your Precious Name, Amen

WHEN WERE YOU MOST AWARE OF GOD'S SOVEREIGNTY IN YOUR LIFE?:

_____

_____

_____

_____

_____

PERSONAL

Thank You, God, that You are...personal.

PERSONAL

O Lord, You have searched me and known me. You know my sitting down and my rising up; You understand my thought afar off. You comprehend my path and my lying down, And are acquainted with all my ways. For there is not a word on my tongue, But behold, O Lord, You know it altogether...(Psalm 139:1-4)

It's humbling to know that the God who created the heavens and the earth cares about me and the details of and in my life.

Yesterday, I had several hours of quiet time with the Lord... and then went on to read some required material for a class I am taking. I came to a portion of the book, and it was like I could feel the Lord gently nudging me...as He revealed some "tactics" of mine. He opened my eyes to some unhealthy ways I have been going about getting desired behavior from my children. I kept reading, and it was like the author knew one of my children and was using him as an example in his book. It was not a pleasant example, and I was pretty taken aback. I'll admit that I was sad and a bit discouraged.

A few hours went by and I noticed one of my other kiddos being unusually helpful and agreeable, so I complimented him. He left the room and came back crying. He couldn't get his words out, as I asked what was wrong. He asked me to sit with him and, through tears, said, "I can feel God working in me." (I'm sure you know what I did next...*bawls like a baby*) He then told me how he wants to go to heaven, and that he wants others to go too. He described his Sunday school class from the day before. He told me how he doesn't usually dance to the worship songs, but that he had just wanted to praise God— and he didn't care who was watching. (More tears from Mama Bear!)

As we sat there crying, I was able to tell him how my heart had been burdened for one of his siblings…and how God had used him to minister to me, just when I needed it.

My big God reveals to me that He is not a distant God. My big God brings hope when most needed. My big God shows me He is near, present, working, and personal. My big God loves me enough to encourage me in the most intimate of ways. My big God is constantly reminding me that nothing is too small for Him.

PRAISE YOU, MY PERSONAL GOD

Thank You, God...for working and moving in my life. You remind me constantly that You are a God who works in both big and small ways. You encourage me and You strengthen my faith as You reveal Yourself to me in so many different ways. You are a God who cares about even the smallest of details and I am in awe of You. Thank You that I could never deny You because of how You personally speak into my life and heart. Lord, use me to encourage others. Strengthen me, I pray. I seek to honor and glorify You as I love on Your people. Have Your way in me, God.

In Your Precious Name, Amen

HOW HAS GOD SHOWN YOU HE IS PERSONAL AND INVOLVED IN THE DETAILS OF YOUR LIFE?

_____

_____

_____

_____

_____

GOOD

Thank You, God, that You are…good.

GOOD

There's a worship song we often sing, and I can rarely get through it without crying…

♪…from the moment that I wake up…until I lay my head, oh I will sing of the goodness of God…all my life You have been faithful, and all my life You have been so so good…with every breath that I am able, oh I will sing of the goodness of God… Your goodness is running after…it's running after me…with my life laid down, I surrender now…I give You everything…♪

A week before Josh's (and Taylor's) liver transplant surgery, a dear friend sent me a newer version of this song. It was ministering to her in the season she was in and she wanted to share it with me. I listened to it on repeat for days. It's still a go-to when I am applying makeup or in the car alone!

Receiving that song from this particular friend of mine was extra meaningful because she had her own surgery scheduled (for a few weeks after J's and T's)…only hers was a craniotomy to remove an AVM. Do you know how humbling it is when your friend, who's approaching brain surgery, sends you a song about God's goodness? She knew that there were several possible outcomes: a successful surgery, a long/hard recovery, or that the Lord could even take her Home that day.

As many of you know, Josh and Taylor are doing so well! We are beyond grateful that God's good plan for them means Josh is recovering well and that Taylor's body is accepting the new liver, as she is continuing to heal each day!

And as for my sweet friend? Well, she has blown everyone away! Her surgery was successful, her AVM was removed, and she is recovering faster than anyone thought possible.

I know God's plans don't always "feel" good. There have been many times I've prayed for healing, rescuing, etc....and yet He chose to answer in ways I simply could not understand. I couldn't see how the outcomes He chose or allowed were "good."

What I DO know is this: His ways are higher, He sees the big picture, and He has eternal purposes. As He has worked in me through the years, I have come to the place of surrender. I don't have to like it. I just have to trust. He has the final say. He knows best. He is good. Thank You, God!

PRAISE YOU, MY GOOD GOD

Thank You, God…You are so good. You do everything with a plan and a purpose. Lord, remind me of Your goodness each and every day, and especially when things don't feel good. God, You have done so many good things in and through my life. I praise You. What the enemy means for evil, You intend for good. You show Your people that You are always perfect in all of Your ways. You are the God who provides, the God who turns things around, the God who surprises us, and the God who makes a way for us. Oh Jesus, I love You. You are so good to me…

In Your Precious Name, Amen

HOW HAS GOD SHOWN HIS GOODNESS IN YOUR LIFE?

_____

_____

_____

_____

_____

ENOUGH

Thank You, God, that You are...enough.

ENOUGH

Last night, during communion, we sang:

♪Christ is my reward and all of my devotion...Now there's nothing in this world that could ever satisfy...Christ is enough for me...Christ is enough for me...Everything I need is in You...everything I need...♪

On the way home, another song came on, and we sang:

♪Jireh, You are enough...I will be content in every circumstance...forever enough...more than enough...♪

You may find it odd that I consulted Webster (in my favorite 1828), but in doing so, I discovered that "enough" means: sufficiently; in a quantity or degree that satisfies; satisfies desire or gives content...

Psalm 90:14 says: *Oh, satisfy us early with Your mercy, That we may rejoice and be glad all our days!*

Psalm 107:9 says: *For He satisfies the longing soul, And fills the hungry soul with goodness.*

Psalm 145:16 says: *You open Your hand and satisfy the desires of every living thing.*

The verses that describe God being "enough" and "sufficient" and "the One who satisfies" are endless!

I love how we can run to Him at any given time, and He's never going to come up short or empty-handed. The fridge will always be full; the cupboards always stocked! Christ will always BE enough and He always SUPPLIES enough (most of the time—more than enough).

We are reminded in 2 Corinthians 12:9 that: *My grace is sufficient for you, for My strength is made perfect in weaknesss.*

God's well will never run dry! Whether it's grace, mercy, contentment, strength, peace...He longs to satisfy us. He wants us to need Him...and nothing more.

We can grasp at tangible and temporal things, but they'll always leave us wanting more. Nothing in this world will ever be "enough." Our fleshly satisfaction is fleeting. He is the only One who can fill us. As we draw ever closer to the Lord, we will want more and more of Him.

The best part is that there will never be a day where He says, "That's it! No more!" He will always always always give enough. Have enough. Be enough.

More of You, God. Less of me. You are (more than) enough for me.

PRAISE YOU, MY SUFFICIENT GOD

Thank You, God…that You are enough for me. You are my portion and my supply. You are all-sufficient and You are much more than just enough. You give abundantly. You supply my needs according to Your glorious riches. Your grace is enough for me…and I rely upon it daily. Nothing in this world can ever satisfy. You alone can bring contentment and satisfaction, for You are the Living Water and the Bread of Life! I praise You…

In Your Precious Name, Amen

HOW HAS GOD SHOWN HIS SUFFICIENCY IN YOUR LIFE?

_____

_____

_____

_____

_____

ABLE

Thank You, God, that You are…able.

ABLE

As of late, the Lord has been reminding me that He is ABLE.

I have the privilege of being a part of the prayer team at church. After service—hurting, broken, scared, discouraged, hopeful, expectant people come forward to share their requests and receive prayer. Often, I am left speechless. As they share their hearts, I have internal dialogues with the Lord. 'Lord, this is all too much. You have to give me the words to pray. This is so heavy. I know You can. I know You're able!'

There are two verses from the book of Jeremiah that He puts on my heart time and time again…

Ah, Lord God! Behold, You have made the heavens and the earth by Your great power and outstretched arm. There is nothing too hard for You. (Jeremiah 32:17)

Behold, I am the Lord, the God of all flesh. Is there anything too hard for Me? (Jeremiah 32:27)

(P.S. That's a rhetorical question. We already know the answer is NO! Nothing's too hard for Him!)

Webster tells me that able is described as: having competent power and strength; competent fortitude; sufficient knowledge or skill.

Does not the Creator of the heavens and the earth, the God of all flesh, have competent power, strength, knowledge, and skill?

The answer will always be a resounding YES. Praise!

As I sit here typing this up, a song comes to mind. He likes to use dictionaries and music to speak to me...

♪God is able...He will never fail...He is Almighty God... Greater than all we seek...Greater than all we ask...He has done great things...Lifted up...He defeated the grave...Raised to life...Our God is able...In His name we overcome...For the Lord our God is able...God is with us...God is on our side... He will make a way...Far above all we know...Far above all we hope...He has done great things! ♪

I used to struggle greatly with the fact that, though He is able, our paths and outcomes can often look differently than we had hoped. Over the past year, I have felt Him doing a work in my heart. There's a stirring in within me. A desire to encourage others that there is always hope— in our able God.

As long as we have breath, we can hang onto hope, cling to His truths and promises, and rest in the fact that NO-thing is too hard for Him!

PRAISE YOU, MY ABLE GOD

Thank You, God…You are my able Father, protector, provider, and healer. There is nothing that is too hard for You. I praise You for all of the ways You have answered my prayers. I thank You for saying "no" to many prayers I have prayed, because You had a better plan. God, You can do anything. Help me to surrender all to You and to submit to Your plan and to Your will. All of my hope and trust is in You and You alone!

In Your Precious Name, Amen

HOW HAS GOD SHOWN HIS ABILITY IN YOUR LIFE?

_____

_____

_____

_____

_____

AVAILABLE

Thank You, God, that You are...available.

AVAILABLE

We live in a world where:

*It's hard to get a "live" person on the phone
*We get put "on hold"
*Waiting in lines can seemingly take forever
*Reservations and appointments have to be made

Often times, our schedules are so busy that even carving out time with our closest friends can be tricky!

I often take for granted the fact that I have a God who is available and accessible 24/7!

I will lift my eyes to the hills— From whence comes my help? My help comes from the Lord, Who made heaven and earth. He will not allow your foot to be moved; He who keeps you will not slumber. Behold, He who keeps Israel shall neither slumber nor sleep. (Psalm 121:1-4)

I don't know about you, but it's pretty humbling for me to know that my God is always available.

I don't have to stand in a line to wait to talk to Him.

He doesn't put me on hold because He has a high volume of calls, or because He's too busy talking to someone else.

He doesn't squeeze me into His tight schedule.

He doesn't pencil me in on His calendar, to then cancel on me because something [better] comes up.

He doesn't oversleep, get bored while I'm talking, or check His watch.

I realize I am describing a lot of human tendencies...but the point is this: our God is always available, He will never turn us away, and we don't have to wait for access to Him.

How many times have I overslept (or hit the snooze button) and then skipped out on quiet times with Him? How often do I overcommit or fill my calendar to the point where there's no time to spend in prayer, or in the Word, throughout the day? How long do I leave my God on the other end of the proverbial phone...on hold or waiting while I talk to someone else?

I am so thankful that Jeremiah 33:3 (a.k.a. God's phone number) tells me: *Call to Me, and I will answer you, and show you great and mighty things, which you do not know.*

The Lord is near to all who call upon Him, To all who call upon Him in truth...(Psalm 145:18a)

Never too tired. Never too busy. Never closed.
Always available. Always accessible.

Thank You, Lord!

PRAISE YOU, MY AVAILABLE GOD

Thank You, Lord Jesus....that You are always accessible and available. You desire that I would come to You, converse with You, talk to You, rely upon You. Thank You that You never slumber nor sleep and that I can come boldly before Your throne. Holy Spirit, convict...when I choose other people or things, as You wait for me to choose You. May You be my first thought of the day and the last thought before I fall into sleep each night. Thank You for sending Jesus...my Savior who tore the veil and made a way for me to always have access to You—the Holy One.

In Your Precious Name, Amen

HOW HAS GOD BEEN AVAILABLE IN YOUR TIME OF NEED?

_____

_____

_____

_____

_____

PATIENT

Thank You, God, that You are...patient.

PATIENT

The Bible has a lot to say about God's patience (and longsuffering) toward us. As I was looking up verses, I was reminded that He is patient with both believers and unbelievers.

For those of us IN Christ:

He works on/in each of us in different ways, at different times. We fail. He picks us up and washes us off. We become discouraged when we don't see change. He moves in unseen ways...patiently working to grow and refine us. We sin against Him. He continues to love us, desiring for us to spend forever with Him.

For those NOT (yet) IN Christ:

2 Peter 3:9 says: *The Lord is not slack concerning His promise, as some count slackness, but is longsuffering toward us, not willing that any should perish but that all should come to repentance.*

The days continue to get darker, yet, our God continues to patiently wait— so that more souls will be saved from eternal damnation. He doesn't strike dead those who mock Him, hate Him, refuse Him...rather, He desires that they turn to Him...to accept His free gift of grace and eternity with Him.

As a Christ follower, there is this desire to just be in heaven, of course...but there's also a crying out to God to "just wait a little longer." "Have a little more patience, Lord!"

On a human level— it's heartbreaking when people we love don't choose Christ. We pray fervently for them to have a change of heart. In Acts 1:8, we are commissioned to share the Good News wherever we go.

I can't even imagine how God must feel. Oh, how His heart grieves and breaks...when the very people He created to spend eternity with Him dig their heels in and deny Him.

I am so thankful for the Lord's patience towards me. When I truly sit and think upon His patience, I see my lack thereof. As soon as I begin to get down on myself, He lifts my chin and reminds me of His love and longsuffering for me.

I am grateful that God isn't finished with me yet! I am beyond thankful that He is always at work in each of us.

I am blessed by His patience and willingness to "wait" for me to grow and, by His great love and mercy, for those not yet rooted in Him.

He is perfect Love. Love is patient.

PRAISE YOU, MY PATIENT GOD

Thank You, Lord...for being a patient Father. Thank You for your long-suffering toward me and toward all of humanity. I am stubborn and stiff-necked...I turn aside, I wander, and I am tempted to go astray. You are always patient with me...in Your pruning and refining of me. Thank You that You are patient toward those who do not yet know You. You desire all to come to a saving knowledge of You. Teach me to have a patient heart, and to learn through all You allow in my life. In my waiting, Lord, help me to turn to You, to seek You in all circumstances, and to become more like You. I love You...

In Your Precious Name, Amen

HOW HAS GOD SHOWN HIS PATIENCE IN YOUR LIFE?

_____

_____

_____

_____

_____

WONDERFUL

Thank You, God, that You are…wonderful.

WONDERFUL

I can't count how many times I've simply stood...

Awestruck. Overwhelmed. Astonished. Perplexed.

The God who created waterfalls, rainbows, clouds, sunsets, rivers, lakes, sea creatures, canyons, oceans, mountains, the solar system, trees, flowers, land animals...also created YOU and ME. Every intricate part of the human body...

Psalm 139:13-14 read: *For You formed my inward parts; You covered me in my mother's womb. I will praise You, for I am fearfully and wonderfully made; Marvelous are Your works, And that my soul knows very well.*

I am constantly amazed by God and His wonderful designs!

A few months ago, I learned that the human liver is the only organ that doesn't age...and that it can regenerate. When Josh met with the surgeon, we learned that not only would Josh's liver (the 35% he got to keep) regenerate, but that the portion Taylor received would also grow! Learning things like this makes me want to shake people who don't believe there's an Intelligent Designer...

Webster defines amazing as: adapted to excite wonder or admiration; exciting surprise; astonishing

The way I see it: amazing and wonderful go hand in hand!

The most awe-inspiring thing to me is that this most amazing and wonderful God...the One who created the hummingbird's heart to beat 1,260 times per minute, who brings forth rain, who made the sun to give light and warmth, and who designed the liver to regenerate...loves me so much that He sent His only Son...

For unto us a Child is born, Unto us a Son is given; And the government will be upon His shoulder. And His name will be called WONDERFUL, Counselor, Mighty God, Everlasting Father, Prince of Peace. (Isaiah 9:6)

Born for me. Bled for me. Died for me. Rose for me!

...that I might live for Him.

Glorify Him (in word and deed).

Praise Him (with every breath).

Stand in awe of Him.

Spend eternity with Him.

He is wonderful and I am full of wonder!

PRAISE YOU, MY
WONDERFUL GOD

Thank You, Lord…You are so wonderful. I am constantly in awe of You and of Your works and ways. You always reveal Yourself to Your people in Your creation. We look upon the beauty You made— to bring us joy and to give us understanding of Your great love for us. I marvel at You and Your handiwork. I humbly bow to You and to Your will, for I know that You are full of splendor. The heavens declare Your glory and I will too! Praise You, God…

In Your Precious Name, Amen

HOW MANY WONDERFUL THINGS CAN YOU LIST THAT HAS GOD DONE FOR/ SHOWN YOU?

_____

_____

_____

_____

_____

OMNIPRESENT

Thank You, God, that You are…omnipresent.

OMNIPRESENT

Last night, I went into my nine year old's room to pray with him and to hug him good night. He told me how he kept having scary thoughts. As he described his fears, I was able to remind him of a portion of Scripture that I had read yesterday.

Where can I go from Your Spirit? Or where can I flee from Your presence? If I ascend into heaven, You are there; If I make my bed in hell, behold, You are there. If I take the wings of the morning, And dwell in the uttermost parts of the sea, Even there Your hand shall lead me, And Your right hand shall hold me. If I say, "Surely the darkness shall fall on me," Even the night shall be light about me; Indeed, the darkness shall not hide from You, But the night shines as the day; The darkness and the light are both alike to You. (Psalm 139:7-12)

As I was paraphrasing, my son nodded and said, "I've been thinking about God's omnipresence..."

We continued talking about how we don't ever need to be afraid because He is always with us! There's nowhere we can go that our God won't be.

Webster puts it very simply: "present in all places at the same time."

There are multiple locations in the Bible that speak of God's omnipresence, and of His promise to never leave us.

Be strong and of good courage, do not fear nor be afraid of them; for the Lord your God, He is the One who goes with you. He will not leave you nor forsake you. (Deut. 31:6)

And the Lord, He is the One who goes before you. He will be with you. He will not leave you nor forsake you; do not fear nor be dismayed. (Deut. 31:8)

God's omnipresence is consoling and comforting to the believer: bringing peace, rest, and even holy conviction (when we are where we ought not be)! Yet, the fact that God is everywhere all at once is a source of discomfort and unrest for the unbeliever who: denies God/His existence, tries to run from Him, and/or doesn't believe He is always with them. There can even be an escapism mentality as they try to distract themselves from reality.

I am thankful my boy can lay his head on his pillow, knowing God is there— promising never to leave him!

I am beyond thankful for this attribute ascribed solely to God!

PRAISE YOU, MY OMNIPRESENT GOD

Thank You, my Savior...You are always with me. You are everywhere, all at once. I cannot fully comprehend how You are always present but I am so thankful that I can live in peace. I do not have anything to fear because You are with me. You promise to never leave me nor forsake me. Your Word says I cannot flee from Your Spirit or from Your presence and I find great comfort in that. Lord, thank You that You see all and that You hold me in the palm of Your hand. I give You honor and glory...

In Your Precious Name, Amen

WHEN ARE/WERE YOU MOST AWARE OF GOD'S OMNIPRESENCE?

_____

_____

_____

_____

_____

GRACIOUS

Thank you, God, that You are...gracious.

GRACIOUS

Every time I truly think upon God's grace: His "favor," "good will," "kindness," and His "free, unmerited love" for me...I am humbled and undone.

I am reminded of my own flesh— my flaws, flubs, fears, and failures. Our humanity means our grace is lacking, and we are in need of a Savior. Basically, we need His grace like we need air.

God is our gracious Father...our perfect parent.

I experience God's grace— moment by moment, hour by hour, day by day. I am called to give that grace to those around me as well. To pour it out as I receive it.

Being a mom poses many opportunities to give grace. Every time I lose my patience or I discipline out of anger or frustration, I think: 'This is NOT how my God parents me.'

My God is... *"merciful and gracious, slow to anger, and abounding in mercy."* (Psalm 103:8)

My God is... *"Gracious and righteous; Yes, our God is merciful."* (Psalm 116:5)

My God's grace...is what saves!

For the grace of God that brings salvation has appeared to all men, teaching us that, denying ungodliness and worldly lusts, we should live soberly, righteously, and godly in the present age, looking for the blessed hope and glorious appearing of our great God and Savior Jesus Christ... (Titus 2:11-13)

I will get to experience heaven— eternity with Him— not because I'm "good enough"...but because He is gracious toward me, and has adopted me as His own.

My God's grace...is my source of strength and it's what sustains me!

And He said to me, "My grace is sufficient for you, for My strength is made perfect in weakness." Therefore most gladly I will rather boast in my infirmities, that the power of Christ may rest upon me. (2 Cor. 12:9)

It is ONLY by His amazing grace that I am: alive, saved, sustained, strengthened, and heaven bound!

♪Amazing grace...how sweet the sound...that saved a wretch like me! ♪

Thank You for Your grace, Lord.

PRAISE YOU, MY GRACIOUS GOD

Oh Jesus...You are full of grace. You give so abundantly. Your grace is not only sufficient but it never runs out. Lord, I want You to increase in my life, while my flesh decreases. Work in me, mold me, prune me...and make me into one who is full of grace, I pray. As I experience Your amazing, never-ending well of grace, please compel and propel my heart to align with Yours. Thank You for giving me so much more than I deserve. Thank You for Your endless supply of grace and mercy in my life. I exalt You today.

In Your Precious Name, Amen

HOW HAS GOD DISPLAYED
HIS GRACE TO YOU?

_____

_____

_____

_____

_____

MERCIFUL

Thank You, God, that You are...merciful.

MERCIFUL

Grace is something undeserved but given, while mercy is not giving something deserved.

These words come up a lot in our household, as we parent our four children!

Our God is so gracious and merciful, that He continues to forgive our offenses, time and time again. He exercises tenderness and He is compassionate toward us. He treats us with mildness and is daily "disposed to pity offenders and to forgive their offenses." (Webster)

Years ago, a friend told me that she did not like the fact that her children's school was teaching her kids that they were little sinners. We don't like to hear it, do we? We don't enjoy introspection, where we have to come to grips with the fact that we offend God daily.

One thing is for sure: We need His forgiveness and we would be in hell for eternity, if not for His mercy and grace.

I am so thankful that "His mercies are new every morning!" As long as we are here on earth, He gives mercy: abundantly, freely, undeservedly.

I love Micah 7:18, which says:
Who is a God like You, Pardoning iniquity and passing over the transgression of the remnant of His heritage? He does not retain His anger forever, Because He delights in mercy.

It's amazing that we don't ever have to be afraid of God!

Hebrews 4:15-16 tell us:
For we do not have a High Priest who cannot sympathize with our weaknesses, but was in all points tempted as we are, yet without sin. Let us therefore come boldly to the throne of grace, that we may obtain mercy and find grace to help in time of need.

As a child of His, I am called (and commanded) to be merciful, compassionate, forgiving, and tender.

But love your enemies, do good, and lend, hoping for nothing in return; and your reward will be great, and you will be sons of the Most High. For He is kind to the unthankful and the evil. Therefore be merciful, just as your Father is also merciful. (Luke 6:35-36)

I was pondering the irony of: How many times has the Lord been merciful to me...while I am literally in the act of withholding mercy upon others? Lord, work in me. More of You. Less of me.

Thank You for Your mercy!

PRAISE YOU, MY MERCIFUL GOD

Thank You, God...for Your mercy. Thank You that You do not give me what I deserve. I deserve hell and yet, You saw fit to send Your Son to take my sin upon Himself. My inheritance is heaven! I don't deserve it...I have done nothing to earn eternity with You. You love me so much that You are merciful toward me, and You long for me to show that same mercy to others as well. Your Word says that Your mercy abounds and that it never fails me. I am forever grateful. I love You, Lord...

In Your Precious Name, Amen

IN WHAT WAY(S) HAS GOD BEEN MERCIFUL TO YOU?

_____

_____

_____

_____

_____

MAJESTIC

Thank You, God, that You are…majestic.

MAJESTIC

This might be one of my most favorite attributes of God! As I was scrolling through my photos recently, I began searching "sunsets." I came to a photo I had taken on our 20th anniversary trip to the Maldives. The fiery sky, the orange hues reflecting off of the Indian Ocean, how the sky meets the water along the horizon. Wow! (...and the pictures I have don't even do it justice!)

I remember standing there in that beautiful, captivating moment— trying to take it all in. Never wanting to forget...

As a matter of fact, there are certain "time stamps" in my mind— places I've gotten to visit, explore, and experience... moments and scenes that took my breath away— forever embossed in my mind. A worship song or verse will come to mind, and wherever I am when those moments hit, I quietly worship my majestic Creator.

As I ponder God's majesty, I can't help but think about humanity...

When I look at this photo, I see things "man" made as well. We: copy, produce, re-create. We build majestic "things" and we can even design beautiful spots and locations amidst our Creator's creation.

BUT...these things are all manufactured and/or fabricated. Humans cannot create sunsets, oceans, clouds, colorful fish, and so on.

As I looked up synonyms for majestic, I found: spectacular, stately, splendid, glorious, beautiful, grand, magnificent, excellent, breathtaking...

One thing that often comes to mind when I'm overcome by God's majesty and splendor is: This is only a glimmer of what I will see in heaven. It cannot even compare to what awaits me!

Not only are His creations majestic, but His name alone is!

LORD, our Lord, How majestic is Your name in all the earth! (Psalm 8:9, NASB)

Our Lord's name is majestic, and all that He has created for us to behold is too!

Yours, O LORD, is the greatness, The power and the glory, The victory and the majesty; For all that is in heaven and in earth is Yours; Yours is the kingdom, O LORD, And You are exalted as head over all. (1 Chronicles 29:11)

I will meditate on the glorious splendor of Your majesty, And on Your wondrous works. (Psalm 145:5)

Lord, You are Majesty! You are the Maker of majestic creations! I will praise You forever!

PRAISE YOU, MY MAJESTIC GOD

Thank You, God...for the beauty of Your majesty. I stand in complete reverence of You. Whether I am: watching the sun set or the stars twinkle in the clear night sky, smelling flowers You created in all sorts of vibrant colors, studying the human eye and the brilliance of it, hearing a baby's cry or the sound of leaves rustling in the breeze, tasting a juicy strawberry or drinking cold water on a hot day...I am in awe of the things You have created for me to experience, enjoy, and behold. I praise You— for You are full of splendor. You are my beautiful God, my Elohim...

In Your Precious Name, Amen

WHEN (AND WHERE) WERE YOU MOST AWARE OF GOD'S MAJESTY?

_____

_____

_____

_____

_____

GENEROUS

Thank You, God, that You are...generous.

GENEROUS

Isn't our God so generous? Without Him, we would HAVE nothing. We would BE nothing.

He generously:

- Fills our lungs with air, allowing us life on His earth (Acts 17:25)
- Causes the earth to keep spinning on its axis (1 Chron. 16:30-31, Ps. 24:1)
- Gives abundant grace (2 Cor. 9:8, Heb. 4:16)
- Provides endless forgiveness (Eph. 1:7)
- Clothes and feeds us (Matt.6:25, Phil. 4:19)
- Bestows spiritual gifts upon us (1 Cor. 12, 1 Peter 4:10)
- Gives wisdom when we ask (James 1:5)

…and the list goes on and on.

But— the most generous gift He ever gave was His Son!

For God so loved the world that He gave His only begotten Son, that whoever believes in Him should not perish but have everlasting life. (John 3:16)

Because of the gift of Jesus— His death and resurrection— I also receive the gift of eternal life!

For the wages of sin is death, but the gift of God is eternal life in Christ

Jesus our Lord. (Romans 6:23)

I often take God's generous gifts for granted. I heard a quote years ago and I've never forgotten it: "What if you woke up today with only what you thanked God for yesterday?"Wow. Powerful, isn't it?

Growing up, I was extremely selfish, especially towards my younger sister. If I let her borrow something, my "generosity" came with so many stipulations that it was rarely even worth it for her. We can laugh about it now, but it wasn't funny at the time (and it drove my mom crazy). Now, when I see my children acting selfishly, I cringe. I can't help but be reminded of how I once was. I am thankful that age, maturity, and spiritual growth have revealed to me that everything I have is from God!

Every good gift and every perfect gift is from above, and comes down from the Father of lights, with whom there is no variation or shadow of turning. (James 1:17)

When I truly understand that everything is His, I won't have a tight grip on, or a closed fist around, what is "mine." I'll want to *"sow bountifully"..."for God loves a cheerful giver."* (2 Corinthians 9:6-9)

♪ You give life…You are love…You bring light to the darkness… You give hope…You restore…It's Your breath in our lungs… So we pour out our praise to You only! ♪

You are a generous Giver! You've given us SO much. We praise You! More like You each day, we pray…

PRAISE YOU, MY GENEROUS GOD

Thank You, God...for Your generosity. Everything I have and everything I am is from You. You give graciously and abundantly and I am grateful. Lord, work in me and create within me a heart of gratitude. I never want to take people, moments, or things for granted...as is my human nature and tendency. Forgive me for the times I have not thanked You and for the times I have "expected" from You. You give liberally and without expectation. Make me into one who does the same. I love You, my generous Giver...

In Your Precious Name, Amen

HOW HAS GOD BEEN GENEROUS TO YOU?

_____

_____

_____

_____

_____

OMNIPOTENT

Thank You, God, that You are...omnipotent.

OMNIPOTENT

As a follower of Christ, I rest in the fact that my God is: Almighty; possessing unlimited power; all powerful (Webster's 1828)

All of my faith, hope, and trust is in Him- the One who even the wind and waves obey!

...And suddenly a great tempest arose on the sea, so that the boat was covered with the waves. But He [Jesus] was asleep. Then His disciples came to Him and awoke Him, saying, "Lord, save us! We are perishing!" But He said to them, "Why are you fearful, O you of little faith?" Then He arose and rebuked the winds and the sea, and there was a great calm. So the men marveled, saying, "Who can this be, that even the winds and the sea obey Him?" (Matt.8:24-27)

The hard part is that we often don't understand His ways, His plans, or the things He allows. More often than not, evil seems to "win." However, His Word reminds me that He already has the final say...the ultimate victory!

When God answers (or doesn't answer) my prayers in the way(s) I had hoped, I have to remember— my life is but a vapor, and my faith is in the Maker of heaven and earth! (James 4:14)

Reading the book of Job can be difficult, as Job questions and laments for many chapters. Then, in chapter 38, God begins to reveal His omnipotence to Job. Question after rhetorical question, God [righteously] puts him in his place.

I have to chuckle because I'm reminded of years ago when I would listen to Dr. Laura on the radio. I used to cringe as she would give it to her callers- real straight! Hear me: I am in NO WAY relating our all-powerful God to a fallible human being! Rather, it's a silly way for me to think of how we tend to ramble and complain. Then the "authority" answers! Though I would never call in to her, I've got the Ultimate Authority on speed dial!

NO thing and NO one can interrupt, thwart, or prevail against the Almighty One!

I know that You can do everything, And that no purpose of Yours can be withheld from You. (Job 42:2)

He knows best.

He has a plan and a purpose in everything!

For the Lord of hosts has purposed, And who will annul it? His hand is stretched out, And who will turn it back? (Is. 14:27)

PRAISE YOU, MY OMNIPOTENT GOD

Thank You, God...for You are mighty and powerful. No one and nothing can stop You. You are the ultimate Authority. Every created thing bows at Your command. Thank You that I can trust You. Everything You plan, will, or allow serves Your kingdom purposes. You even tell us in Your Word that the things the enemy intends for evil— You mean for good. Lord, please help me to willingly submit to You in all things. You hold the world in the palm of Your hand and You hold me. I praise You that Your hand is righteous, omnipotent, all-powerful...

In Your Precious Name, Amen

HOW (OR WHEN) HAS GOD SHOWN YOU HIS OMNIPOTENCE?

_____

_____

_____

_____

_____

TRUSTWORTHY

Thank You, God, that You are...trustworthy.

TRUSTWORTHY

Trust = confidence; reliance or resting of the mind on the integrity, veracity, justice, friendship or other sound principle of another

There have been a few times recently that I've heard my younger two discuss their fear of the dark with one another. Last week, while I was praying with Keaton at bedtime, he was struggling with scary thoughts. We had a good discussion about how we can call upon the name of Jesus. We can simply speak His name and the darkness trembles.

Just now, as I was looking through my Bible, I came to Isaiah 50:10...

Who among you fears the Lord? Who obeys the voice of His Servant? Who walks in darkness and has no light? Let him TRUST in the name of the Lord and rely upon his God.

I can't wait to share this verse with the kids when they wake up...and in the future, when they're scared/afraid.

A few nights ago, I heard Keaton tell Quinn... "When you're scared, just say Jesus' name. It really works! I just did it." He had just come back inside, after taking some cans to our recycling bin in the dark backyard. (If you're a parent, you know how incredible it is when our kids "get it!")

Like our kids trust us for their next meal and to get them where they need to go, so we can trust our perfect Father— who loves us with an everlasting love.

He is trustworthy. He has never failed us and He never will. Man fails us, disappoints, and breaks promises. BUT our God does not!

Whether it's actual illumination we need...or a "shedding of light on" a specific matter or decision- He will do it!

Behold, God is my salvation, I will trust and not be afraid; For YAH, the Lord, is my strength and song; He also has become my salvation. (Isaiah 12:2)

Not only can we trust Him with our very lives, but we can trust Him enough to surrender all to Him!

In Him you also trusted, after you heard the word of truth, the gospel of your salvation; in whom also, having believed, you were sealed with the Holy Spirit of promise... (Eph. 1:13)

Trust in the Lord with all your heart, And lean not on your own understanding; In all your ways acknowledge Him, And He shall direct your paths. (Prov. 3:5-6)

...in God I trust!

PRAISE YOU, MY TRUSTWORTHY GOD

Thank You, God...that I can place all of my hope and trust in You. Sometimes it's hard for me to lay everything at Your feet, as I cast my cares and burdens upon You...and yet I know— that's the best way to surrender. I can fall into You, for You will never let me down. You will always always always be worthy of my trust, my affection, and my allegiance. Lord, work in me...may I not live in fear, worry, or doubt. I know You are in control and You are sovereign, good, and provident. I give it all to You— the One who has numbered all of my days, knows every part of me, and has a plan and a purpose in all things. Praise You, God...

In Your Precious Name, Amen

HOW HAS GOD SHOWN YOU HE IS WORTHY OF YOUR TRUST?

_____

_____

_____

_____

_____

JEALOUS

Thank You, God, that You are…jealous.

JEALOUS

I realize that sounds like an odd thing to thank God for…but, humanly speaking: if my husband had no problem with me stepping out of our marriage vows and into a "relationship" with another man— that would be weird (and not okay). My husband shouldn't want to share me or my affections.

This simple illustration gives me a deeper understanding of God's jealousy for me…

He wants ALL of me.

He doesn't want to share my heart.

He doesn't want to be shoved into a tiny spot in my heart, or collecting dust in a corner of my mind. He doesn't want to sit in a crowded room, vying for my attention and devotion.

A song we sometimes sing at church comes to mind…

♪You won't relent until You have it all…My heart is Yours…I'll set You as a seal…upon my heart…As a seal upon my arm…For there is love, that is as strong as death…Jealousy demanding as the grave…And many waters cannot quench this love…Come be the fire inside of me…Come be the flame upon my heart… Come be the fire inside of me…Until You and I are one…We are one…I don't wanna talk about You like You're not in the room…I wanna look right at You…wanna sing right to You…♪

There's a powerful, little booklet called My Heart, Christ's

Home. It's a reminder that God is everywhere: waiting for us to notice and "remember" Him. We go through the rooms of our homes and often pass Him by, giving our time and allegiance to other people/things. Our church bookstore has a children's version of the booklet. I started crying, as I read it to my kids a few days ago...convicted, heartbroken.

God wants to be the centrality of my very being!

"Every aspect of my existence was meant to be filled with the glory of God. Everything I think, every decision I make, every word I speak was meant to be shaped by a humble acknowledgement of His claim on my life." (P.D. Tripp)

...for you shall worship no other god, for the Lord, whose name is Jealous, is a jealous God. (Exodus 34:14)

My worship, my allegiance, my focus, time, and talents...may they all be Yours, Lord.

Thank You that You won't settle for just a piece of my heart. You won't relent until You have it all.

PRAISE YOU, MY JEALOUS GOD

Thank You, God...that You want all of me. Thank You that You don't want to share me with other loves, but that You want to have first place in my heart and life. Lord, my heart is prone to wander from You. I love You, yet I desire to love You more... and in a deeper way. Thank You that though You are jealous for me and my affections, Your love for me never fades. Thank You that You are constant and constantly in love with me. You know everything about me, because You created me...and You long for me to know You and desire You. Keep me from turning aside to other "gods." Deepen my love for You, as You work in and through me.

In Your Precious Name, Amen

WHEN HAS GOD SHOWN YOU HE IS JEALOUS FOR YOUR AFFECTIONS?

_____

_____

_____

_____

_____

GREAT

Thank You, God, that You are...great.

GREAT

Song lyrics flood my mind as I write:

♪...all the earth will shout Your praise...our hearts will cry... these bones will sing...great are You, Lord! ♪

♪...Your name is great and Your heart is kind...for all Your goodness I will keep on singing...♪

♪...then sings my soul, my Savior God to Thee...how great Thou art! ♪

♪...Oh Jesus, our Savior, Your name lifted high...Oh God, You have done great things...♪

I love words. I enjoy searching for synonyms almost as much as I enjoy looking up definitions in my 1828. (Does that make me a nerd? If so, I'm okay with it!)

There are over two hundred synonyms for the word great, but some of my favorites are: considerable, enormous, awesome, astounding, immense, tremendous, vast...and put very simply— BIG.

A childhood song comes to mind:

♪ My God is so great...so strong and so mighty...there's nothing my God cannot do! ♪

I love Psalm 145:3, which says:

Great is the Lord, and greatly to be praised; And His greatness is unsearchable.

We will never be able to grasp, contain, or fully fathom His greatness! However, we can declare His greatness...and share the great things He has done in our lives.

...and I will declare Your greatness... (Psalm 145:6b)

O Lord my God, You are very great: You are clothed with honor and majesty... (Psalm 104:1)

As believers we are strengthened and encouraged when we share the great things He has done and non-believers can't really argue about His greatness in my life! Others may deny His hand in their own, but no one can debate me on the ways God has personally shown me how big He is! I will not stop sharing about my great God! He is constantly working and moving—and He is coming back!

I am...*looking for the blessed hope and glorious appearing of our great God and Savior Jesus Christ!* (Titus 2:13) Are you?

My heart, like Mary's, sings: *For He who is mighty has done great things for me, And holy is His name.* (Luke 1:49)

Thank You, God! Not only is Your name great, but You have done great things...and You are not done yet!

PRAISE YOU, MY GREAT GOD

Thank You, God…You are not only good, but You are great! You do great things! You reveal Your greatness always! I praise You for the great things You have done. I have seen Your greatness personally— time and time again. When I think back over my life, I cannot deny Your hand or Your tremendous goodness. Lord, I want to proclaim to all of those around me that You are a BIG God, worthy of our adoration. You are awesome and You astound us. You work outside of time and boundaries. You answer our prayers. Thank You for your never-ending greatness. I will give You glory and honor all my days…

In Your Precious Name, Amen

HOW HAS GOD SHOWN HIS GREATNESS IN YOUR LIFE?

_____

_____

_____

_____

_____

ACTIVE

Thank You, God, that You are...active.

ACTIVE

I have had the privilege of praying with many people over the years, after church services. I don't know the people who come forward personally, and recently there have been many hefty requests. It's always awesome to see how the Lord shows up, and to experience the Holy Spirit directing my prayers for these strangers.

A few weeks ago, I was praying with a woman for an impossible situation in her life. While I was praying, the Lord reminded me of how He had worked a miracle for us during our daughter's adoption process. I was then able to share with this woman after I prayed. (The crazy thing is that Quinn has been home for over six years and I had honestly "forgotten" about this thing God had done. He spurred my memory as I prayed with her.)

Through prayer, I am always reminded of how God is working. Actively in the unseen. Busy behind the scenes. Operating in unimaginable ways!

A few days ago, I got out my personal copy of Come & Adore (my devotional published in 2020). Flipping through, I reread my chicken scratch from last year. Names, journal entries, and prayer requests fill the book. Taylor D. and her parents are named all throughout, as I had been praying daily for her healing. I was blown away. Humbled. Awestruck. None of us could have imagined what God had in store. He was actively making a way for Taylor's transplant even then! Preparing hearts. Providing. Guiding. Leading the way. Opening doors.

Our dear friends' son has battled leukemia for three years. His name is also throughout my book. Today— Mikah is cancer free! He took his last chemo pill earlier this week, and is having his port removed as I type.

On the way home from church the other night, I turned on a song I love...

♪ He is up to something
♪ God is doing something right now
♪ He is healing someone
♪ He is saving someone
♪ God is doing something right now
♪ He is moving mountains
♪ Making a way for someone
♪ God is doing something right now...

One generation shall praise Your works to another, And shall declare Your mighty acts. (Psalm 145:4)

As long as I have breath, I will tell of the amazing things He has done and IS doing. He IS active and working. He IS moving and making a way.

At the time of publication (2023), Mikah is undergoing chemo treatments due to a relapse of his cancer. Please pray with me for him and his family!

PRAISE YOU, MY ACTIVE GOD

Thank You, God...You are alive and You are active in my life! You constantly encourage my heart, just when I need it most. You show me that You are a God who is working in and through me. You remind me that You are moving in the unseen and that I am to trust that You know best. I want my faith to be an active faith and I humbly ask You to embolden me, to strengthen me, and to equip me. I want to be a doer and not just a hearer of Your word. I want all to know that You are the Living God! Thank You, Father, that You love me so much and that You never slumber nor sleep. Thank You for hearing the cries of my heart and for answering according to Your will. In You, we live and move and have our being...and we praise You for that!

In Your Precious Name, Amen

HOW HAS GOD SHOWN YOU HE IS ACTIVELY INVOLVED IN YOUR LIFE?

_____

_____

_____

_____

_____

WISE

Thank You, God, that You are...wise.

WISE

Now to the King eternal, immortal, invisible, to God who alone is wise, be honor and glory forever and ever. Amen. (1 Timothy 1:17)

The ONLY wise One will impart godly wisdom to us! All we have to do is ask...

If any of you lacks wisdom, let him ask of God, who gives to all liberally and without reproach, and it will be given to him. (James 1:5)

Raise your hand if you're sick of seeing pillows, cups, and shirts with messages like: Follow Your Heart or Do What Makes You Happy stamped, embossed, or embroidered on them?! (*me raising my hand*)

Our hearts are deceitfully wicked (Jer. 17:9) and they will lead us astray. We need to ask for God's perfect wisdom so that we don't become like the world, which is saturated in foolishness.

Webster tells us wisdom is..."having knowledge; hence, having the power of discerning and judging correctly, or of discriminating between what is true and what is false; between what is fit and proper, and what is improper..."

It's amazing that the God of the universe, who knows all and sees all, can be trusted because He alone is wise. He sees the end from the beginning. He knows what is best because His wisdom is infinite!

My heart was convicted years ago, upon hearing a teaching on

Isaiah 55. In so many words, the pastor was spanking us for ever thinking we "know better" than God. Every time we think or say:

"Seems a tad harsh, God!"
"I don't understand why God would allow that!"
"Why would God choose to do (or not do) that?!"
"If I were God, I would've..."

...we are essentially elevating ourselves; internally placing our feeble, human brains above God!

Isaiah 55:8-9 tells us:
"For My thoughts are not your thoughts, Nor are your ways My ways," says the Lord. "For as the heavens are higher than the earth, So are My ways higher than your ways, And My thoughts than your thoughts."

We cannot fully comprehend the depths of God's limitless wisdom!

Oh, the depth of the riches both of the wisdom and knowledge of God! (Romans 11:33a)

Jeremiah 10:7b says:
For among all the wise men of the nations, And in all their kingdoms, There is none like You!

Thank You, God— for Your Word which gives wisdom, and that You alone are wise!

PRAISE YOU, MY WISE GOD

Thank You, God...for You alone are wise. You alone are worthy of honor and glory and praise. You see all, You know all, and You are sovereign over all. It was by wisdom that You founded the earth. Your ways are higher and beyond understanding, so God, I ask You to help me fully trust— even when I don't understand. You tell me in Your Word that You give Your wisdom liberally to those who ask. It is Your wisdom from above that I desire, not the world's empty and shallow ways. I seek You and You alone. Please quiet other "voices" that are not Yours. May Yours be the loudest and the only one that I long for and listen to. Praise You, my wise and loving Father...

In Your Precious Name, Amen

HOW HAS OUR WISE GOD IMPARTED HIS WISDOM TO YOU?

_____

_____

_____

_____

_____

HOLY

Thank You, God, that You are...holy.

HOLY

The Bible repeatedly speaks of God's holiness.

Who is like You, O Lord, among the gods? Who is like You, glorious in holiness, Fearful in praises, doing wonders? (Exodus 15:11)

No one is holy like the Lord, For there is none besides You, Nor is there any rock like our God. (1 Samuel 2:2)

And one cried to another and said: "Holy, holy, holy is the Lord of hosts; The whole earth is full of His glory!" (Isaiah 6:3)

Webster defines holy as: perfectly just and good; perfectly pure; immaculate and complete in moral character...

He goes on to say: "We call a man holy when his heart is conformed to some degree to the image of God, and his life is regulated by divine precepts."

I love this call to consecration! Is my heart conformed to His image? Is my life regulated by His Word?

Yes, we fail.
Yes, we sin.
Yes, we fall short of the glory of God.

BUT God is holy, pure, just— and He calls us to be as well! Our lives should look different after we become His.

Therefore gird up the loins of your mind, be sober, and rest your hope fully upon the grace that is to be brought to you at the revelation of Jesus Christ; as obedient children, not conforming yourselves to the former lusts, as in your ignorance; but as He who called you is holy, you also be holy in all your conduct, because it is written, "Be holy, for I am holy." (1 Peter 1:13-16)

I have lots of talks with my kids about their hearts and their conduct. I desire for them to live holy lives, pleasing to the Lord. The Lord then has lots of talks with me about my heart and conduct. The closer I draw to Him, the more my heart is conformed to His.

I will not enter into heaven because I lived a moral life, rather my love for a holy God should stir within me a desire to be set apart for His glory.

Pursue peace with all people, and holiness, without which no one will see the Lord. (Hebrews 12:14)

♪ What heart could hold the weight of Your love? And know the heights of Your great worth? What eyes could look on Your glorious face...shining like the sun? You are holy, holy, holy! God most high and God most worthy! ♪

God, You are holy and I will pursue You all my days!

PRAISE YOU, MY HOLY GOD

Thank You, God...You are holy, holy, holy...and worthy of all my praise and exaltation! You are my Lord God Almighty and You alone are worthy. God, You are pure and just and You long for me to live a life that is holy, consecrated, and set apart. I pray that my life would reflect Your goodness and Your holiness. Lord, I desire to put away my flesh my sinful desires, and choices that would grieve You— so that I might live a holy, pure, and righteous life in You. Lord, I long to be an upright ambassador for Your kingdom. May my time in Your presence feel like holy ground and may I guard it fiercely and regard it highly. I give You my life, Holy One...

In Your Precious Name, Amen

HOW HAS GOD REVEALED HIS HOLINESS TO YOU?

_____

_____

_____

_____

_____

RIGHTEOUS

Thank You, God, that You are...righteous..

RIGHTEOUS

Righteousness, when applied to God, means: "the perfection of holiness of His nature; exact rectitude…"

I love how Webster states: "Perfect rectitude belongs only to the Supreme Being."

Since rectitude isn't a word I use everyday (or ever), I had to look it up:

"…in morality, rightness of principle or practice; uprightness of mind; exact conformity to truth."

God's Word doesn't pull any punches…there is none righteous, no, not one…

Romans 3 goes on to tell us that it's not through the law, but by Jesus' blood, that God demonstrates His righteousness.

♪ My hope is built on nothing less…Than Jesus' blood and righteousness…I dare not trust the sweetest frame…But wholly lean on Jesus' name! ♪

For He made Him who knew no sin to be sin for us, that we might become the righteousness of God in Him. (2 Corinthians 5:21)

God not only imparts to us righteousness, but calls us to live righteously and uprightly.

Psalm 45:7 tells us *"You love righteousness and hate wickedness…"*

God also calls us to put on righteousness. It's part of our daily uniform! (Eph. 6:14)

I don't know about you, but I want to live an "upright, upstanding, worthy, virtuous, decent, and ethical" life…before my holy and perfect Father. Of course, I am going to mess up and sin. I will fall short and I will fail…but I will daily ask Him to clothe me in His righteousness.

"And if anyone sins, we have an Advocate with the Father, Jesus Christ the righteous." (1 John 2:1b)

Thank You, God, that You are righteous.
Thank You that by Jesus' blood, I am made righteous.

Fear not, for I am with you; Be not dismayed, for I am your God. I will strengthen you, Yes, I will help you, I will uphold you with My righteous right hand. (Isaiah 41:10)

Thank You that I have nothing to fear and that You uphold me.

For I am not ashamed of the gospel of Christ, for it is the power of God to salvation for everyone who believes, for the Jew first and also for the Greek. For in it the righteousness of God is revealed from faith to faith; as it is written, "The just shall live by faith." (Romans 1:16-17)

Thank You that I can share You with others and live it, Lord!

PRAISE YOU, MY RIGHTEOUS GOD

Thank You, God…You are my righteous Savior, Father, and Lord. You are perfect— and perfect in all of Your ways. Thank You that I can rest in Your righteousness, knowing You are always good and sovereign over all. Jesus, I thank You for Your blood, which has not only cleansed me and covered me, but has imparted righteousness to me. You call me to be holy and to put on righteousness, living in a way that is pleasing to You. Work in my heart and in my life, God, I pray. Don't allow the things of this world to pull me away from You, but rather, mold me and make me to be a bold witness for You. Thank You for Your perfect and priceless gift of righteousness…

In Your Precious Name, Amen

HOW HAS GOD'S RIGHTEOUSNESS COMPELLED YOU TO LIVE UPRIGHTLY?

_____

_____

_____

_____

_____

STRONG

Thank You, God, that You are...strong.

STRONG

So often, in prayer, God's strength and might come to mind. I am reminded of countless times He has shown Himself mighty on my behalf!

Recently, I was praying with a woman. She's experiencing chronic pain in her right hand. As I held her hand and prayed, the Lord brought to mind the Scriptures that speak of His right hand.

You have a mighty arm; Strong is Your hand, and high is Your right hand. (Psalm 89:13)

Job speaks of God's strength:
If it is a matter of strength, indeed He is strong. (Job 9:19)

Not only did God create the world WITH His hand, but He holds it IN His hand.

That's some serious strength and might, right there!

With whom My hand will be established; My arm also will strengthen him. (Psalm 89:21)

It's God's hand that holds the power to: destroy, stop, redeem, save, carry, protect, strengthen...

And He said to me, "My grace is sufficient for you, for My strength is made perfect in weakness. Therefore most gladly I will rather boast in my infirmities, that the power of Christ may rest upon me. Therefore I take pleasure in infirmities, in reproaches, in needs, in persecutions, in distresses, for Christ's sake. For when I am weak, then I am strong." (2 Cor. 12:9-10)

Personally, I find freedom in knowing that I am weak, but that He is strong. I cannot accomplish anything in my own strength...but *"I can do all things through Christ who strengthens me!"* (Phil. 4:13)

I loathe the little t-shirts that read "Girl Power." If I was to make a shirt, it would read: "God Powered!" Amen?

My heart cries:
I will love You, O Lord, my strength. The Lord is my rock and my fortress and my deliverer; My God, my strength, in whom I trust; My shield and the horn of my salvation, my stronghold. (Psalm 18:1-2)

Don't you just breathe a sigh of relief as you read those descriptions of our strong and mighty God?

It is God who arms me with strength, And makes my way perfect. (Psalm 18:32)

The Lord is my light and my salvation; Whom shall I fear? The Lord is the strength of my life; Of whom shall I be afraid? (Psalm 27:1)

Thank You, God! I have nothing to fear because You are my strength!

PRAISE YOU, MY STRONG GOD

Thank You, God...You are strong! Nothing is too hard for You! You are mighty! You defeated death, You rose victoriously, and You have the final say. You tell me to be still and know that You are God. Lord, thank You that I have nothing to fear because You are powerful and able, and I can leave everything in Your capable hands. You desire that I surrender all to You. I am weak, but You, God, are strong. Your strength is made perfect in my weakness, and for that reason, I rejoice that I can do nothing apart from or without You. Lord, continue to remind me of Your strength, Your ability, and Your providence. I thank You that You are my Refuge, my Fortress, and my Strong Tower...

In Your Precious Name, Amen

HOW HAS GOD SHOWN HIMSELF MIGHTY IN YOUR LIFE?

_____

_____

_____

_____

_____

LOVING

Thank You, God, that You are...loving.

LOVING

"The hope of every sinner does not rest in theological answers but in the love of Christ for His own." (Paul David Tripp)

I am no Tozer or Lewis, so forgive me if this doesn't make sense...but I would suggest to you that pretty much every other attribute of God stems from His great love for us.

He is personal, generous, merciful, gracious, majestic, etc....all because of His perfect love for us!

For God, so loved the world that He gave His only begotten son, that whoever believes in Him shall not perish, but have everlasting life. (John 3:16)

The Lord wants us to love others the way that He loves us!

This is My commandment, that you love one another as I have loved you. Greater love has no one than this, than to lay down one's life for his friends. (John 15:12-13)

We are called to love God first, and then we are called to love His people. And we are not only to love—but to sacrificially give of ourselves. That's the kind of love God has for us...

But God demonstrates His own love toward us, in that while we were still sinners, Christ died for us. (Romans 5:8)

Love should be what propels us and what compels us...what motivates us and drives us.

Beloved, let us love one another, for love is of God; and everyone who loves is born of God and knows God. He who does not love does not know God, for God is love. (1 John 4:7-8)

We can't fool, God. He knows when our love for Him and for others is genuine. He knows when we are spending time with him to simply check the box on our list of to-dos, or when our hearts are fully invested.

PRAISE YOU, MY LOVING GOD

Thank You, God...for Your perfect love. Jesus, thank You for saving me...by giving Your very life and Your blood upon the cross for me. Thank You that Your love is unconditional, and that there is nothing I can do to separate myself from You/it. Thank You that, though I don't deserve Your love, You gave all for me. Thank You that I get to spend eternity with You! Lord, I love You but I want to love You more deeply. I want to love Your people better. Work in me and give me a heart like Yours: one that loves, one that serves, and one that gives selflessly and freely. I give my life to You, and I ask that You have Your way in me. Give me a pure, undefiled, and genuine agape love...

In Your Precious Name, Amen

HOW HAS GOD SHOWN YOU UNCONDITIONAL LOVE?

_____

_____

_____

_____

_____

PRAISEWORTHY

Thank You, God, that You are...praiseworthy.

PRAISEWORTHY

Enter into His gates with thanksgiving, And into His courts with praise. Be thankful to Him, and bless His name. (Psalm 100:4)

Last night was a family service at church. I'll be honest and share that they're not usually my favorite. When the kids were younger, it felt like too much "work" to get them to sit quietly for ninety minutes, but as they've grown, they have more of an understanding and are able to sit and listen.

Last night, as we worshiped...I was overcome with gratitude. My kids were sandwiched between me and Josh. My heart was full as we sang...

♪ Bless the Lord, O my soul...I'll worship Your holy name...♪

♪ I'll throw up my hands and praise You again and again... 'cause all that I have is a hallelujah...♪

♪ Holy...holy...are You Lord God Almighty...worthy is the Lamb...You are holy! ♪

After worship, a video was played. Testimony after testimony of what God has done in people's lives...we listened to them give thanks— through grief, loss, healing, restoration, joy.

I am pretty emotional anyway, but it would be hard for anyone to sit through those stories and not want to throw up their hands in praise to our amazing and worthy Lord!

As we took communion, we were reminded of the reason we praise. Our God sent His Son to be that perfect sacrifice— the Lamb upon the cross...that if we confess Him as Lord and Savior, we might live in eternity with Him!

But you are a chosen generation, a royal priesthood, a holy nation, His own special people, that you may proclaim the praises of Him who called you out of darkness and into His marvelous light. (1 Peter 2:9)

He's alive and working— we have much to praise Him for. Amidst loss, sadness, grief...and in joy and elation— He is always worthy! Our hearts can always praise.

Bless the Lord, O my soul; And all that is within me, bless His holy name! (Psalm 103:1)

Rejoice always, pray without ceasing, in everything give thanks; for this is the will of God in Christ Jesus for you. (1 Thess. 5:16-18)

Praise the Lord! For it is good to sing praises to our God; For it is pleasant, and praise is beautiful. (Psalm 147:1)

PRAISE YOU, MY PRAISEWORTHY GOD

Thank You, God...You are so worthy of all of my praise! Lord, I want to honor You with my life, my heart, and my lips. You alone deserve all the glory and honor and praise! Let everything that has breath praise Your name...and let me be the first to exalt You. When I rise, may Your praise be on my lips. When I lie down at night, may I honor You with a heart of gratitude and thanksgiving. As I go about my day, may I be mindful of ALL You have done for me and given me and may that result in a heart of praise and adoration for You. Forgive me for the times I have a spirit of "complaining" and "grumbling." Shift my gaze and focus to You! Oh how good You are and how worthy You are of all my heartfelt praise.

In Your Precious Name, Amen

HOW CAN YOU PRAISE OUR MOST WORTHY GOD TODAY?

_____

_____

_____

_____

_____

UNCHANGING

Thank You, God, that You are…unchanging.

UNCHANGING

Humans are so wishy-washy, so fickle...we change our minds constantly. We can't decide what color to paint our walls, which drink to order at Starbucks, or what we want for dinner.

Our wants and desires are fleeting. Trends and fads come and go and it's hard to keep up!

I am so thankful that, though I live in an ever-changing world, I serve a God who never changes!

But You are the same, And Your years will have no end. (Psalm 102:27)

I love how God's Word lays it out plainly for us in Hebrews...

Jesus Christ is the same yesterday, today, and forever. (Heb. 13:8)

Though my decisions, choices, and circumstances may vary and fluctuate...and though there will be times of instability or uncertainty...

I can rest, knowing my future lies in the hands of a: constant, stable, steady, enduring God!

Everything I have and everything I am comes from my unchanging Father!

Every good gift and every perfect gift is from above, and comes down from the Father of lights, with whom there is no variation or shadow of turning. (James 1:17)

I've gone through many stages in my life, and though I don't remember life without Christ, my priorities have shifted over time. My desire is that my love for the Lord will continue to change— for the better. The closer I draw to Him, the more I understand that His love for me never changes. He doesn't ever love me more or less.

His Word will always remain.
He was here before time began and He will reign forever.
His covenants and promises are eternally true.
His character? Constant.
His will? Immutable.

Thus God, determining to show more abundantly to the heirs of promises the immutability of His counsel, confirmed it by an oath, that by two immutable things, in which it is impossible for God to lie, we might have strong consolation, who have fled for refuge to lay hold of the hope set before us. This hope we have as an anchor of the soul, both sure and steadfast, and which enters the Presence behind the veil. (Hebrews 6:17-19)

I don't know about you— but I am tethering myself to the Unchanging Anchor, the Everlasting One, the Ancient of Days!

PRAISE YOU, MY UNCHANGING GOD

Thank You, God...that You are unchanging and immutable. I am so thankful that You are the same yesterday, today, and forever. I rejoice in the fact that though my thoughts, decisions, feelings, and actions change— You do not. Your are my constant source of stability. You never fail me. Thank You that under Your wings I can find refuge. You have always been and You always will be. Thank You that I can have eternal life— with my unchanging and everlasting Father God. Lord, guide me in every decision. Lead me in every thought. May I never cease to make You the number one priority in my life. I long to draw nearer to You, Jesus. I ask You— immovable God— to move me closer to You and Your heart.

In Your Precious Name, Amen

HOW HAS GOD DEMONSTRATED HIS UNCHANGING CHARACTER TOWARD YOU?

_____

_____

_____

_____

_____

MARVELOUS

Thank You, God, that You are…marvelous.

MARVELOUS

I will praise You, O Lord, with my whole heart; I will tell of all Your marvelous works. (Psalm 9:1)

Our family loves to travel and we have been blessed to see some amazing places. Exactly two years ago, the six of us spent a week in the Azores, on a small island called Terceira.

Through a random (inexpensive) Travelzoo deal, we were able to take our kids on their most favorite vacation! It's one that they still talk about nearly everyday! (A few of them even talk about living there one day…)

This small island full of rolling hills, lava rock, lush green valleys, forests, beaches, caves, islets, and volcanoes made for the most incredible week of exploring God's creation.

You can't help but marvel as you're standing inside a wet cave or watching steam vent from a volcano.

Marvelous means: wonderful, improbable, incredible, excellent, splendid…(Webster, 1828)

In doing my synonym search, I found: astounding, astonishing, sensational, breathtaking, extraordinary…

Remember His marvelous works which He has done, His wonders, and the judgments of His mouth…(1 Chronicles 16:12)

Not only has God created marvelous things for us to behold

and enjoy, but He has done marvelous things!

But as for me, I would seek God, And to God I would commit my cause— Who does great things, and unsearchable, marvelous things without number. (Job 5:8-9)

For You are great, and do wondrous things; You alone are God. (Psalm 86:10)

Oh, sing to the Lord a new song! For He has done marvelous things; His right hand and His holy arm have gained Him the victory. (Psalm 98:1)

Several times, we are told to remember!

Remember His marvelous works which He has done, His wonders, and the judgments of His mouth... (Psalm 105:5)

One way I "remember" is by journaling. Sadly, there are so many times I've looked back to entries from years ago— only to be reminded of amazing things God did— that I had somehow "forgotten." When He causes me to recall a memory or reminds me through my own words, I am astounded!

He blows my mind, He rocks my world, He takes my breath away...as I marvel at Him and His wonders!

PRAISE YOU, MY MARVELOUS GOD

Thank You, God...You are a marvelous God! I stand in awe and in wonder of You...often speechless. You are amazing and wonderful and full of splendor! Your works and ways are breathtaking, unsearchable, and beyond comprehension. I love that about You, my glorious God! You can be known but You cannot be fully "figured out." Your ways are higher than our ways! I will praise You always and I will proclaim You and Your wondrous ways to those around me. Lord, I vow to remember the great things You have done...and I commit to marveling at You, Your creation, and Your beauty! Thank You, my extraordinary Maker!

In Your Precious Name, Amen

WHAT MARVELOUS WORKS OF GOD CAN YOU THANK HIM FOR TODAY?

_____

_____

_____

_____

_____

JUST

Thank You, God, that You are...just.

JUST

He is the Rock, His work is perfect; For all His ways are justice, A God of truth and without injustice; Righteous and upright is He.
(Deuteronomy 32:4)

According to Webster, just means: impartial, allowing what is due; true; founded in truth and fact; faithful...

Some synonyms for just are "equitable" and "unbiased."

Job tells us...*Surely God will never do wickedly, Nor will the Almighty pervert justice.*

Every time I go to search the Word on a different attribute of God, I am further reminded of how dark and lost this world is. Our world doesn't like (or want) true justice. We can't honestly say we are an impartial people. Is the world full of upright and honest humans? I wish. I tend to become discouraged by the moral decay; the decline of humanity.

Nearly two years ago, Josh and I were Christmas shopping when we were witnesses to grand theft. People have stolen personal property from us as well. When these things happen, I want "justice to be served!"

As a nation and a world, we watch injustices happen almost daily. Dehumanizing, horrible, tragic, heartbreaking things... that break the heart of God (and His people).

I know that the Lord will maintain the cause of the afflicted, and justice for the poor. Surely the righteous shall give thanks to Your name; The upright shall dwell in Your presence. (Psalm 140:12-13)

It's hard to witness afflictions and turmoil...especially when we feel helpless. (We can always pray— and there is power in praying to our just God!)

Therefore the Lord will wait, that He may be gracious to you; And therefore He will be exalted, that He may have mercy on you. For the Lord is a God of justice; blessed are all those who wait for Him. (Isaiah 30:18)

When I am tempted to question, I have to remember that He's not only just but patient and merciful.

Romans and Colossians both speak of the day when God will repay wrong. What a scary day for those in opposition to God. I pray for them to submit and surrender their lives to Him.

Praise You, my perfectly just God!

PRAISE YOU, MY JUST GOD

Thank You, God…for You are just. You see it all! You see every injustice. You are aware of every "unfair" thing. You will always reign Supreme and You will avenge all evil. I thank You that You did for me what I couldn't do for myself. You made a way for me, a wretched sinner, to be justified and to be made righteous. You, O Righteous Judge, are patient and kind. You are merciful and long-suffering, yet You are also holy and perfectly just. You will [make] right every wrong and You will mend everything that is broken. Father, I praise You that You are perfect and just, and that You are the Perfect Judge who reigns over all. I long for the day I am with You in eternity…

In Your Precious Name, Amen

WHEN HAS GOD SHOWN YOU THAT HE IS JUST?

_____

_____

_____

_____

_____

OMNISCIENT

Thank You, God, that You are...omniscient.

OMNISCIENT

Webster's description of omniscience is: having universal knowledge or knowledge of all things; infinitely knowing; all-seeing...

The Bible repeatedly speaks of how God knows the hearts of men. He knows our intent, our motive, our every thought....

Would not God search this out? For He knows the secrets of the heart. (Psalm 44:21)

O Lord, You have searched me and known me. You know my sitting down and my rising up; You understand my thought afar off. You comprehend my path and my lying down, And are acquainted with all my ways. For there is not a word on my tongue, But behold, O Lord, You know it altogether... (Psalm 139:1-4)

Your eyes saw my substance, being yet unformed. And in Your book they all were written. The days fashioned for me, When as yet there were none of them. (Psalm 139:16)

All of Isaiah 40 is amazing— reminding us of how BIG, powerful, and great God is!

Not only does our God know everything about us: when we were formed, the day we are to be born, the day we will leave this earth, and everyday in between...but He knows all of His creations well!

Lift up your eyes on high, And see who has created these things, Who brings out their host by number; He calls them all by name, By the greatness of His might and the strength of His power; Not one is missing. (Isaiah 40:26)

Have you not known? Have you not heard? The everlasting God, the Lord, the Creator of the ends of the earth, Neither faints nor is weary. His understanding is unsearchable. (Isaiah 40:28)

God's omniscience is beyond our understanding and we will never be able to fully grasp it.

My parents, my sister, my children, and my husband know me better than anyone else. They get the good, the bad, and the ugly.

How mind-blowing and humbling it is for me to really sit and think about the fact that God knows EVERY part of me! Not just the good, the bad, and the ugly...but the secret and the unspoken as well.

He still loves me, chooses me, uses me, and wants me.

God's knowledge and understanding of all things give me great comfort. I don't have to know everything because I am held in the hands of the One who does!

Thank You, Omniscient One!

PRAISE YOU, MY OMNISCIENT GOD

Thank You, God...for You are the all-knowing, omniscient One. You know every part of me and yet, You love me with an unfailing and everlasting love. You see all of me. You know all of my thoughts, plans, and even the motives of my heart. You know every word of mine, before it is ever on my tongue. Thank You, Lord, that You still desire a relationship with me. Thank You that, though You know the state of my sinful heart, You allow me to be used for Your kingdom purposes. I want to deepen my relationship with You, my Abba. I don't have to know everything— but I long to know You more! In You is true, everlasting life and peace and a deep abiding joy!

In Your Precious Name, Amen

HOW HAS GOD DEMONSTRATED HIS OMNISCIENCE IN YOUR LIFE?

_____

_____

_____

_____

_____

ETERNAL

Thank You, God, that You are…eternal.

ETERNAL

...everlasting, never-ending, undying, endless...are just a few more words to describe our eternal God, His Word, and His kingdom!

The Lord shall reign forever and ever. (Exodus 15:18)

The eternal God is your refuge, And underneath are the everlasting arms... (Deuteronomy 33:27a)

Your kingdom is an everlasting kingdom, And Your dominion endures throughout all generations. (Psalm 145:13)

The grass withers, the flower fades, But the word of our God stands forever. (Isaiah 40:8)

I love that my God has always been, and that He always will be.

Before the mountains were brought forth, Or ever You had formed the earth and the world, Even from everlasting to everlasting, You are God. (Psalm 90:2)

You, O Lord, remain forever; Your throne from generation to generation. (Lamentations 5:19)

Not only is God everlasting and eternal, but He created us to be as well! Of course— He is the only One to reign and rule, and to have everlasting dominion over His kingdom...but God gave us souls— and those are eternal. God didn't create robots. He gave us free will. We can choose eternity— with or without

Him.

Romans 1:20 speaks of how God's invisible attributes are clearly seen...

For since the creation of the world His invisible attributes are clearly seen, being understood by the things that are made, even His eternal power and Godhead, so that they are without excuse...

None of us has an excuse for not choosing to spend eternity with our Everlasting God! He makes Himself seen and known.

Most assuredly, I say to you, he who believes in Me has everlasting life. (John 6:47)

If we are His sheep, we follow Him and hear His voice...

And I give them eternal life, and they shall never perish; neither shall anyone snatch them out of My hand. (John 10:28)

The sun shall no longer be your light by day, Nor for brightness shall the moon give light to you; But the Lord will be to you an everlasting light, and your God your glory. (Isaiah 60:19)

To Him be the glory and the dominion forever and ever. Amen. (1 Peter 5:11)

Thank You for allowing me to choose eternity with You, God... Alpha and Omega! Your kingdom has no end!

PRAISE YOU, MY ETERNAL GOD

Thank You, God...that You are eternal. You are the everlasting God! Your kingdom has no end! You have always been and You always will be. Thank You for creating me to be an eternal being, Lord. Thank You for allowing me to have eternal life with You one day. I long for the day I get to see You face to face... worshiping You for eternity. Jesus, thank You for shedding Your blood for me. I ask You to save those who are lost, those who reject Your name, and those who are in opposition to You. You are willing that none should perish, but that all would have eternal life in You.

In Your Precious Name, Amen

HOW CAN YOU THANK GOD FOR HIS GIFT OF ETERNAL LIFE?

_____

_____

_____

_____

_____

TRUE

Thank You, God…that You and Your Word
are true!

TRUE

About a year ago, one of our children kept falling into the sin/ trap of lying. Out of all of the sins that can be committed against me (and ultimately, God)…lying is the very worst. This particular child would sneak something, try to hide it, then lie about it. The "good" thing is that this child was/is a terrible liar. Every single time a lie was told, Josh and I knew. Recently, a dear friend and I were talking about how: though the sinner can control the sin, he/she cannot control the outcome, the ramifications, or the consequences. Perhaps the worst part of all is that fellowship is broken between the liar and the lied to. Fellowship with our holy God is broken as well, and this should grieve our hearts as it does His.

Then you will know the truth, and the truth will set you free. (John 8:32)

Reading this verse above also reminds me that WHEN we know the Truth, He will set us free!

I am so thankful that God cannot lie! I am so thankful that God's Word is the 100% perfectly inherent truth. He will never trick me, hide things from me, or change His mind. God will always do what He says He will do. He is the only true Promise Keeper! God will never disappoint me, fail me, or lead me astray. The Bible is the only place I can look to find God's truths, and His truths are what keep me on the path that leads to eternal life with Christ— in heaven.

For the law was given through Moses, but grace and truth came through Jesus Christ. (John 1:17)

For the Lord is good; His mercy is everlasting, And His truth endures to all generations. (Psalm 100:5)

Righteousness and justice are the foundation of Your throne; Mercy and truth go before Your face. (Psalm 89:14)

We are living in a day in age where many claim [that we] all should "live your truth"…but this philosophy leads [us] astray. What we need to do is live God's truth! He is the Way, the Truth, and the Life! (John 14:6)

PRAISE YOU, MY TRUE GOD

Thank You, God…that You are true. You are the only Way and You alone are Life! Lord, I desire to walk in Your truth, to live by Your truth, and to speak only Your truth. Lord, I don't want to live according to my emotions, feelings, or anything else that could lead me astray. I thank You that Your Word is the absolute truth and that I can look to You as my ultimate guide and source of light and life.

In Your Precious Name, Amen

WHICH TRUTHS FROM GOD'S WORD CAN YOU CLING TO TODAY?

_____

_____

_____

_____

_____

Photo credit: Jessikah Voong (Truly Blessed Photography)

Kristi and her husband, Josh, have been married for 25 years. They live in Southern California and have four children (and the sweetest Golden Retriever, Gus). The Menashe family has attended Calvary Chapel Chino Hills for 22 years, where they are each involved in various ministries. Kristi is a mentor in the Sister-to-Sister program, facilitates the women's prayer team, and founded Established, the church's homeschool ministry, which she continues to co-lead. Kristi is an avid reader, a logophile, loves squeezing in time for writing, and is obsessed with her American Dictionary of the English Language (Webster, 1828). She loves decorating, design, cooking, and traveling with her family.

Email: kmenashewrites@gmail.com
Visit Kristi on Instagram at: @k.menashe.writes

ACKNOWLEDGEMENTS

To my amazing God— Without You, I am nothing. Thank You for loving me and for using me. My heart is to encourage Your people, to share You with those who don't yet belong to You, and to live as an upright ambassador for Your kingdom. Thank You for the innumerable blessings You've given me (tangible and intangible)...and thank You for saving me. Until You call me Home I will know You and make You known!

To my encouraging and supportive parents, George and Barb— Thank you for raising me to know and love the Lord. Thank you for always spurring me on in my writing, and thank you for always telling me how proud you are. You are not only my parents but my friends, and I am so grateful for you both. I love you so much!

To my beautiful, smart, and creative sister, Kelly— Thank you for always being willing to edit my books! You are one of my biggest cheerleaders and your encouragement and expertise are greatly appreciated. Thank you for answering all of my questions, for catching my mistakes, and for staying up late to read for me. Thank you for your prayers, your support, and for forgiving me for the years I was a selfish brat. I am so thankful to have you as a best friend and confidant.

To my loving family and faithful friends— Thank you for being my "irons." Thank you strengthening me, encouraging me, walking alongside me, praying for me, supporting me, believing in me, and for speaking life into me. I can't imagine how empty this life would be without you in it.

To my incredibly talented friend, Brittany— Without you, all of this would just be letters on a page. Thank you for the many hours you have spent bringing these simple words to life. You have such a gift, and I am forever grateful that you take my writings and make them into beautiful books!

To my anointed and bold pastor, Jack— Thank you for faithfully teaching the Word of God. I have gleaned so much wisdom from your teachings over the past 22 years. Thank you for your boldness, for following the Lord's leading in your life, for not mincing your words, and for never shying away from truth! Thank you that, no matter the size of the congregation, you've always been there for our family. Thank you for the encouragement and support you have given me in my writings over the years.

Song References:

"Promises [Radio Version] Lyrics." Lyrics.com. STANDS4 LLC, 2023. Web. 6 Jun 2023. <https://www.lyrics.com/lyric-lf/6851282/Naomi+Raine/Promises+%5BRadio+Version%5D>.

"Goodness Of God Lyrics." Lyrics.com. STANDS4 LLC, 2023. Web. 6 Jun 2023. <https://www.lyrics.com/lyric-lf/6856617/Jenn+Johnson/Goodness+Of+-God>.

"Christ is Enough Lyrics." Lyrics.com. STANDS4 LLC, 2023. Web. 6 Jun 2023. <https://www.lyrics.com/lyric/29553413/Hillsong/Christ+is+Enough>.

"God is able Lyrics." Lyrics.com. STANDS4 LLC, 2023. Web. 6 Jun 2023. <https://www.lyrics.com/lyric/29133607/Hillsong/God+is+able>.

"Amazing Grace Lyrics." Lyrics.com. STANDS4 LLC, 2023. Web. 6 Jun 2023. <https://www.lyrics.com/lyric/7075321/Darlene+Zschech/Amazing+Grace>.

"Great Are You Lord Lyrics." Lyrics.com. STANDS4 LLC, 2023. Web. 6 Jun 2023. <https://www.lyrics.com/lyric/29333543/All+Sons+%26+Daughters/Great+Are+You+Lord>.

"You Won't Relent Lyrics." Lyrics.com. STANDS4 LLC, 2023. Web. 6 Jun 2023. <https://www.lyrics.com/lyric/19727260/Jesus+Culture/You+Won%27t+Relent>.

"10,000 Reasons (Bless the Lord) Lyrics." Lyrics.com. STANDS4 LLC, 2023. Web. 6 Jun 2023. <https://www.lyrics.com/lyric/23889502/Matt+Redman/10%2C000+Reasons+%28Bless+the+Lord%29>.

"How Great Thou Art Lyrics." Lyrics.com. STANDS4 LLC, 2023. Web. 6 Jun 2023. <https://www.lyrics.com/lyric-lf/197399/Sandi+Patty/How+Great+Thou+Art>.

"Great Things Lyrics." Lyrics.com. STANDS4 LLC, 2023. Web. 6 Jun 2023. <https://www.lyrics.com/lyric/35245617/Phil+Wickham/Great+Things>.

"My God Is So Big Lyrics." Lyrics.com. STANDS4 LLC, 2023. Web. 6 Jun 2023. <https://www.lyrics.com/lyric/8227885/Cedarmont+Kids/My+-God+Is+So+Big>.

"God, Turn It Around [Radio Version] Lyrics." Lyrics.com. STANDS4 LLC,

2023. Web. 6 Jun 2023. <https://www.lyrics.com/lyric-lf/6856284/Jon+Reddick/
God%2C+Turn+It+Around+%5BRadio+Version%5D>.

"Holy Lyrics." Lyrics.com. STANDS4 LLC, 2023. Web. 6 Jun 2023. <https://
www.lyrics.com/lyric/23889503/Matt+Redman/Holy>.

"Cornerstone Lyrics." Lyrics.com. STANDS4 LLC, 2023. Web. 6 Jun 2023.
<https://www.lyrics.com/lyric/26584819/Hillsong/Cornerstone>.

"How Deep the Father's Love for Us Lyrics." Lyrics.com. STANDS4 LLC, 2023.
Web. 6 Jun 2023. <https://www.lyrics.com/lyric/17059007/Selah/How+Deep-
+the+Father%27s+Love+for+Us>.

"Gratitude Lyrics." Lyrics.com. STANDS4 LLC, 2023. Web. 6 Jun 2023. <https://
www.lyrics.com/lyric-lf/5891153/Brandon+Lake/Gratitude>.

"Agnus Dei Lyrics." Lyrics.com. STANDS4 LLC, 2023. Web. 6 Jun 2023.
<https://www.lyrics.com/lyric/5221059/Michael+W.+Smith/Agnus+Dei>.

OTHER BOOKS BY KRISTI

Come & Adore:

It's easy to get caught up in the hustle and bustle of the Christmas season. Come & Adore provides the opportunity to sit and draw near to the One we celebrate. Start your December days with Jesus. Keep focused on Him all month long. Come & Adore is a 25 day advent devotional, with daily Bible readings.

Precious & Pleasant Riches:

Homeschooling is not for the faint of heart! Not everyone is called to teach their children at home, but those who are need support and encouragement along the way. Kristi has a heart to encourage homeschooling parents, through short devotionals and prayers.